Contents

KU-270-466

▶ Short walks

Introduction

View of Grasmere

Walking in the Lake District

The Lake District has a huge variety of terrain for walkers of any age and ability which has helped to make it one of the most popular tourist destinations for over 100 years – low-level lakeside walks, exposed ridge walks, strolls through forests and thrilling mountain walks. Even at the height of summer when the towns and the more popular destinations are teeming with tourists it is still possible to get away from it all and find secluded areas where the magnificent countryside can be enjoyed in relative solitude. Always keep in mind that the weather can change rapidly and a lovely summer's day can quickly change to a torrential downpour especially at higher altitudes. Scafell Pike at 3,209ft (978m) is the highest point in England and at 10½ miles (16.5km) in length Windermere is its longest lake.

Walking is a pastime which can fulfil the needs of everyone. You can adapt it to suit your own preferences and it is one of the healthiest of activities. This guide is for those who just want to walk a few miles. It really doesn't take long to find yourself in some lovely countryside. All the walks are five miles or less so should easily be completed in under three hours. Walking can be anything from an individual pastime to a family stroll, or maybe a group of friends enjoying the fresh air and open spaces of our countryside. There is no need for walking to be competitive and, to get the most from a walk, it shouldn't be regarded simply as a means of covering a given distance in the shortest possible time.

What is the Lake District?

What is seen now in the Lake District still reads historically from north to south. The mountains and hills of Skiddaw Slates which lie in a curving band, from the north to the west, are covered by carboniferous limestones and sandstones nearer the coast, and reappear to the south-west at Black Combe. Because much of this material is shaley and craggy outcrops seldom occur, the fells have angular outlines. Typically of course there is Skiddaw itself (3054ft/931m) with its neighbour

www.harpercollins.co.uk

Copyright © HarperCollins Publishers Ltd June 2010

Original text © John Parker

Collins® is a registered trademark of
HarperCollins Publishers Limited

Mapping generated from Collins Bartholomew
digital databases on the inner front cover and
all walk planning maps

This product uses map data licensed from
Ordnance Survey ® with the permission of the
Controller of Her Majesty's Stationery Office.
© Crown copyright. Licence number 399302

Printed in China

ISBN   978 0 00 735941 7
Imp 001   XJ12505 / UCD

e-mail: roadcheck@harpercollins.co.uk

Blencathra (2847ft/868m). The fells to the west of Derwentwater, Causey Pike and Grisedale Pike, are of the same material, and the rock is also very evident in the fells on the east side of Buttermere, to the north and west around Crummock Water and Loweswater as well as the northern end of Ennerdale Water. There is good soil depth on these rock forms which allows trees and heather to grow naturally.

In the central Lake District, roughly north-east to south-west are the high craggy fells of the Scafells, Great Gable, the Borrowdale fells, as well as Coniston Old Man in the south-west through the Langdales and Bowfell; and eastwards through Helvellyn to High Street. Here, the shallow acidic soils do not support a rich vegetation. The alpine plants are found mainly where springs leach the minerals to the surface. The deeper soils are often covered in bracken, very beautifully coloured in autumn, but useless to the hill farmers' sheep. From another type of rock, formed from fine volcanic sediments in water, come the famous green slate, still quarried and much in demand for its wearing and decorative qualities. It is used for the facings of prestigious buildings. The Honister Slate Mines on the Honister Pass closed in 1986 after three centuries of production. However, it reopened in 1997 as a working slate mine and has become one of the leading attractions in the Lake District.

In the south of the Lake District the soft slates and mudstones produce an acid soil in which trees and forests find root and regenerate quite readily. The typical scenery, much in evidence around Windermere, consists of rounded hills, often with a good deal of tree cover. The Forestry Commission's largest forest, at Grizedale is also in this area.

Before there was a substantial human settlement the whole area was covered in forest. This has been removed over a period of 4,000 years. Much of it was destroyed from early Elizabethan times up to the end of the 19th century to provide charcoal for iron furnaces. The increase in sheep grazing has meant that regeneration has been impossible. Much of the woodland and forest we now see was planted within the last century and a half. The lack of tree cover in many places has accelerated erosion and impoverished the soil.

View of Lake Windermere from Ambleside

Geology

The history of the Lake District over the last 530 million years can be seen in the landscape at the present time.

The oldest rocks are the Skiddaw Slates. These were formed from sediments of gravel, grit and mud laid down in a shallow sea and later subjected to great pressure. Their age is usually put into the Ordovician period some 530 million years ago. Most of this rock series now resembles shale rather than slate. It is minutely jointed and with the action of weather and frost has broken down into small flakes.

After the deposition of the Skiddaw Slates came several millions of years of volcanic action. Lava burst out from below the surface and flowed over the landscape. Explosions threw out hot 'bombs' of rock. Ash settled to huge depths. All this mass of varied material settled to a depth of up to 2 miles (3km) and formed what are known as the Borrowdale Volcanic series of rocks.

After that the whole area was covered by a shallow sea, and erosion material, at first calcareous, then huge amounts of grit and mud settled in layers to a depth of 2½ miles (4km). This was in the Silurian period between 440 and 410 million years ago.

It can be imagined that the then lakeless Lake District consisted of three very thick layers of material each on top of the other. During the Devonian period the earth's crust was subject to extreme movement. The area was thrust upwards into a dome. Each of the rock types reacted differently according to the position of the centre of the thrust. Once the upper layers were fractured, for instance, the more malleable Skiddaw Slate beneath was pushed through to a great height, then hot sandstorms and heavy rains wore down the upper layers. Much of Skiddaw Slates' topmost parts, and a substantial area of the Silurian rocks were swept away. In the central parts the much harder Borrowdale Volcanics were left exposed. Therefore the Skiddaw Slates were left uppermost in the north, the Volcanics in the centre, and the Silurian to the south.

From 345 to 280 million years ago there followed the Carboniferous period. The area was again covered by a sea rich in life. The central part of the district probably remained as an island. The deposits in this sea formed the carboniferous limestone. Subsequently much of this was swept away leaving a rim around the Lake District. The Permo Trias period followed; the area became hot and arid. The desert sands of this time were later solidified into the New Red Sandstone, which again was mainly swept away from the central dome.

The Tertiary period, 65 million years ago brought new upheavals to the planet. This 'Alpine' movement produced the Alps, the Himalayas and the Andes. Again the Lake District's dome was raised high. Fracture lines appeared, in general radiating from the centre, but varying in direction according to the reaction of the material. These formed the basis of the valley patterns we know today.

The next great catastrophe was nearer our own time. About one a half million years ago the climate changed dramatically and the whole of the northern hemisphere was covered in ice. The subsequent movement and melting of the ice hollowed out the valleys and lake beds, and swept away vegetation. The heavy rainstorms later moved any remaining loose material. Thus the dales were sculpted and the lakes were formed.

Wildlife in the Lake District

Because of the huge variety of landscapes to be found in a relatively small area, there are diverse habitats for flora and fauna to thrive. Many different types of grassland, upland heath and mires are designated areas of habitat conservation and protected plant species include juniper and the slender green feather-moss. There are several National Nature Reserves, over 100 Sites of Special Scientific Interest and many other conservation areas.

There are different types of grassland to be found, the species supported being determined by the quality of the soil and the climate. The old fashioned hay meadow is rich in various species of wild flowers and butterflies.

The moorlands of the mountains and fells are carpeted in plant species such as heather and sphagnum moss, commonly called peat moss due to its abundance in bogs and mires. Red grouse can be found on the moorland.

The Lake District supports several endangered species of fish. The vendace was to be found at 4 locations in Britain – two in Scotland and in Bassenthwaite Lake and Derwent Water. However there has not been a recorded sighting in Bassenthwaite since 2001 and they have died out on the Scottish lochs leaving only Derwent Water. The schelly is still to be found in Brothers Water, Haweswater, Red Tarn and Ullswater, and the arctic char, which, although still rare, is a little more commonplace being found in several of the lakes. Cormorant nesting was prevented by repeated disturbance in 1999 and 2000 in Haweswater in an attempt to protect the schelly. Goosander, goldeneye, tufted duck, dipper, grey wagtail and sandpiper can be seen on the lakes and waterways.

The Environment Agency introduced new fisheries bylaws in 2002 regarding the use of freshwater fish as bait in an attempt to protect the fish stocks. The introduction of non-native fish can lead to devastation of native species because of competition for food and spread of disease. A major problem has been found with ruffe which eat the eggs of vendace – they have a long incubation period and are therefore particularly vulnerable.

Numbers of native red squirrels have been dwindling throughout Britain over the last 100 years ever since the grey squirrel arrived from North America. They are more timid and smaller than the greys and lose in the competition for food. A sighting is always an exciting occurrence.

In 2001 ospreys returned to the Lake District after 150 years. A pair spend their winters in Africa but have returned each Spring since then to breed on the hillside around Bassenthwaite Lake. There are now two viewpoints at Dodd Wood north of Keswick, as they recently moved the site of their nest to the opposite side of the lake – a very unusual occurrence as the same site can be used by generations of osprey.

Haweswater was home to England's only pair of Golden Eagles but the female disappeared in 2004 and has not been seen since although sightings of the male are still made.

The Lake District National Park

The Lake District National Park is the largest of the National Parks in England and Wales, with 866 square miles (2242 sq km). The first strongly organised pressure for National Parks and access to mountains came during the 1920s and 1930s when walking and mountaineering became popular pastimes and access to open country in some parts of Britain was much restricted. The outbreak of war postponed progress, and following the reports of John Dower on the need, and the Hobhouse Committee's recommendations on implementation, an Act, The National Parks and Access to the Countryside Act 1949, was passed. 'People need the refreshment which is obtainable from the beauty and quietness of unspoilt country'. The provision for those needs of the people, and the protection from spoilation, were written into the Act.

In many countries of the world National Parks are areas of wilderness hardly influenced by man, and the land of these parks is owned by the nation or state. There is no true wilderness left in Britain. The 'natural' beauty of the landscape reflects the pattern of husbandry, and with so many owning and making a living from the land nationalisation of it was not contemplated. A British National Park is a defined area of unspoilt countryside, usually with some wild, if not wilderness, country, which is specially protected from unsuitable development; public access for its enjoyment is secured, and due regard made for the needs of the local community.

The National Park authority must exercise planning control, but must also provide information and ranger services. In 1969 England's first National Park Visitor Centre was set up at Brockhole in Windermere and is an excellent starting point for exploration of the National Park.

The National Trust and the Lake District National Park Authority work closely with other large landowners, the Forestry Commission and the Water Authority, to provide protected public access unrivalled anywhere

Lake District National Park

else in Britain. It is indeed as Wordsworth said 'a sort of national property' for those 'with eyes to perceive and hearts to enjoy'.

Walking tips & guidance

Safety

As with all other outdoor activities, walking is safe provided a few simple commonsense rules are followed:

- Make sure you are fit enough to complete the walk;

- Always try to let others know where you intend going, especially if you are walking alone;

- Be clothed adequately for the weather and always wear suitable footwear;

- Always allow plenty of time for the walk, especially if it is longer or harder than you have done before;

- Whatever the distance you plan to walk, always allow plenty of daylight hours unless you are absolutely certain of the route;

- If mist or bad weather come on unexpectedly, do not panic but instead try to remember the last certain feature which you have passed (road, farm, wood, etc.). Then work out your route from that point on the map but be sure of your route before continuing;

- Do not dislodge stones on the high edges: there may be climbers or other walkers on the lower crags and slopes;

- Unfortunately, accidents can happen even on the easiest of walks. If this should be the case and you need the help of others, make sure that the injured person is safe in a place where no further injury is likely to occur. For example, the injured person should not be left on a steep hillside or in danger from falling rocks. If you have a mobile phone and there is a signal, call for assistance. If, however, you are unable to contact help by mobile and you cannot leave anyone with the injured person, and even if they are conscious, try to leave a written note explaining their injuries and whatever you have done in the way of first aid treatment. Make sure you know exactly where you left them and then go to find assistance. Make your way to a telephone, dial 999 and ask for the police or mountain rescue. Unless the accident has happened within easy access of a road, it is the responsibility of the police to arrange evacuation. Always give accurate directions on how to find the casualty and, if possible, give an indication of the injuries involved;

- When walking in open country, learn to keep an eye on the immediate foreground while you admire the scenery or plan the route ahead. This may sound difficult but will enhance your walking experience;

- It's best to walk at a steady pace, always on the flat of the feet as this is less tiring. Try not to walk directly up or downhill. A zigzag route is a more comfortable way of negotiating a slope. Running directly downhill is a major cause of erosion on popular hillsides;

- When walking along a country road, walk on the right, facing the traffic. The exception to this rule is, when approaching a blind bend, the walker should cross over to the left and so have a clear view and also be seen in both directions;

- Finally, always park your car where it will not cause inconvenience to other road users or prevent a farmer from gaining access to his fields. Take any valuables with you or lock them out of sight in the car.

Equipment

Equipment, including clothing, footwear and rucksacks, is essentially a personal thing and depends on several factors, such as the type of activity planned, the time of year, and weather likely to be encountered.

All too often, a novice walker will spend money on a fashionable jacket but will skimp when it comes to buying footwear or a comfortable rucksack. Blistered and tired feet quickly remove all enjoyment from even the most exciting walk and a poorly balanced rucksack will soon feel as though you are carrying a ton of bricks. Well designed equipment is not only more comfortable but, being better made, it is longer lasting.

Clothing should be adequate for the day. In summer, remember to protect your head and neck, which are particularly vulnerable in a strong sun and use sun screen. Wear light woollen socks and lightweight boots or strong shoes. A spare pullover and waterproofs carried in the rucksack should, however, always be there in case you need them.

Winter wear is a much more serious affair. Remember that once the body starts to lose heat, it becomes much less efficient. Jeans are particularly unsuitable for winter wear and can sometimes even be downright dangerous.

Waterproof clothing is an area where it pays to buy the best you can afford. Make sure that the jacket is loose-fitting, windproof and has a generous hood. Waterproof overtrousers will not only offer complete protection in the rain but they are also windproof. Do not be misled by flimsy nylon 'showerproof' items. Remember, too, that garments made from rubberised or plastic material are heavy to carry and wear and they trap body condensation. Your rucksack should have wide, padded carrying straps for comfort.

It is important to wear boots that fit well or shoes with a good moulded sole – blisters can ruin any walk! Woollen socks are much more comfortable than any other fibre. Your clothes should be comfortable and not likely to catch on twigs and bushes.

It is important to carry a compass, preferably one of the 'Silva' type as well as this guide. A smaller scale map covering a wider area can add to the enjoyment of a walk. Binoculars are not essential but are very useful for spotting distant stiles and give added interest to viewpoints and wildlife. Although none of the walks in this guide venture too far from civilisation, on a hot day even the shortest of walks can lead to dehydration so a bottle of water is advisable.

Finally, a small first aid kit is an invaluable help in coping with cuts and other small injuries.

Public Rights of Way

In 1949, the National Parks and Access to the Countryside Act tidied up the law covering rights of way. Following public consultation, maps were drawn up by the Countryside Authorities of England and Wales to show all the rights of way. Copies of these maps are available for public inspection and are invaluable when trying to resolve doubts over little-used footpaths. Once on the map, the right of way is irrefutable.

Right of way means that anyone may walk freely on a defined footpath or ride a horse or pedal cycle along a public bridleway. No one may interfere with this right and the walker is within his rights if he removes any obstruction along the route, provided that he has not set out purposely with the intention of removing that obstruction. All obstructions should be reported to the local Highways Authority.

Lake District footpath sign

In England and Wales rights of way fall into three main categories:

- Public Footpaths – for walkers only;

- Bridleways – for passage on foot, horseback, or bicycle;

- Byways – for all the above and for motorized vehicles

Free access to footpaths and bridleways does mean that certain guidelines should be followed as a courtesy to those who live and work in the area. For example, you should only sit down to picnic where it does not interfere with other walkers or the landowner. All gates must be kept closed to prevent stock from straying and dogs must be kept under close control – usually this is interpreted as meaning that they should be kept on a leash. Motor vehicles must not be driven along a public footpath or bridleway without the landowner's consent.

A farmer can put a docile mature beef bull with a herd of cows or heifers, in a field crossed by a public footpath. Beef bulls such as Herefords (usually brown/red colour) are unlikely to be upset by passers by but dairy bulls, like the black and white Friesian, can be dangerous by nature. It is, therefore, illegal for a farmer to let a dairy bull roam loose in a field open to public access.

The Countryside and Rights of Way Act 2000 (the 'right to roam') allows access on foot to areas of legally defined 'open country' – mountain, moor, downland, heath and registered common land. You will find these areas shaded orange on the maps in this guide. It does not allow freedom to walk anywhere. It also increases protection for Sites of Special Scientific Interest, improves wildlife enforcement legislation and allows better management of Areas of Outstanding Natural Beauty.

The Country Code

The Country Code has been designed not as a set of hard and fast rules, although they do have the backing of the law, but as a statement of commonsense. The code is a gentle reminder of how to behave in the countryside. Walkers should walk with the intention of leaving the place exactly as it was before they arrived. There is a saying that a good walker 'leaves only footprints and takes only photographs', which really sums up the code perfectly.

Never walk more than two abreast on a footpath as you will erode more ground by causing an unnatural widening of paths. Also try to avoid the spread of trodden ground around a boggy area. Mud soon cleans off boots but plant life is slow to grow back once it has been worn away.

Have respect for everything in the countryside, be it those beautiful flowers found along the way or a farmer's gate which is difficult to close.

Stone walls were built at a time when labour costs were a fraction of those today and the special skills required to build or repair them have almost disappeared. Never climb over or onto stone walls; always use stiles and gates.

Dogs which chase sheep can cause them to lose their lambs and a farmer is within his rights if he shoots a dog which he believes is worrying his stock.

The moors and woodlands are often tinder dry in summer, so take care not to start a fire. A fire caused by something as simple as a discarded cigarette can burn for weeks, once it gets deep down into the underlying peat.

When walking across fields or enclosed land, make sure that you read the map carefully and avoid trespassing. As a rule, the line of a footpath or right of way, even when it is not clearly defined on the ground, can usually be followed by lining up stiles or gates.

Obviously flowers and plants encountered on a walk should not be taken but left for others passing to enjoy. To use the excuse 'I have only taken a few' is futile. If everyone only took a few the countryside would be devastated. If young wild animals are encountered they should be left well alone. For instance, if a fawn or a deer calf is discovered lying still in the grass it would be wrong to assume that it has been abandoned. Mothers hide their offspring while they go away to graze and browse and return to them at feeding time. If the animals are touched it could mean that they will be abandoned as the human scent might deter the mother from returning to her offspring. Similarly with baby birds, who have not yet mastered flight; they may appear to have been abandoned but often are being watched by their parents who might be waiting for a walker to pass on before coming out to give flight lesson two!

What appear to be harmful snakes should not be killed because firstly the 'snake' could be a slow worm, which looks like a snake but is really a harmless legless lizard, and second, even if it were an adder (they are quite common) it will escape if given the opportunity. Adders are part of the pattern of nature and should not be persecuted. They rarely bite unless they are handled; a foolish act, which is not uncommon; or trodden on, which is rare, as the snakes are usually basking in full view and are very quick to escape.

Map reading

Some people find map reading so easy that they can open a map and immediately relate it to the area of countryside in which they are standing. To others, a map is as unintelligible as ancient Greek! A map is an accurate but flat picture of the three-dimensional features of the countryside. Features such as roads, streams, woodland and buildings are relatively easy to identify, either from their shape or position. Heights, on the other hand, can be difficult to interpret from the single dimension of a map. The Ordnance Survey 1:25,000 mapping used in this guide shows the contours at 5 metre intervals. Summits and spot heights are also shown.

The best way to estimate the angle of a slope, as shown on any map, is to remember that if the contour lines come close together then the slope is steep – the closer together the contours the steeper the slope.

Learn the symbols for features shown on the map and, when starting out on a walk, line up the map with one or more features, which are recognisable both from the map and on the ground. In this way, the map will be correctly positioned relative to the terrain. It should then only be necessary to look from the map towards the footpath or objective of your walk and then make for it! This process is also useful for determining your position at any time during the walk.

Let's take the skill of map reading one stage further: sometimes there are no easily recognisable features nearby: there may be the odd clump of trees and a building or two but none of them can be related exactly to the map. This is a frequent occurrence but there is a simple answer to the problem and this is where the use of a compass comes in. Simply place the map on the ground, or other flat surface, with the compass held gently above the map. Turn the map until the edge is parallel to the line of the compass needle, which should point to the top of the map. Lay the compass on the map and adjust the position of both, making sure that the compass needle still points to the top of the map and is parallel to the edge. By this method, the map is orientated in a north-south alignment. To find your position on the map, look out for prominent features and draw imaginary lines from them down on to the map. Your position is where these lines cross. This method of map reading takes a little practice before you can become proficient but it is worth the effort.

How to use this book

This book contains route maps and descriptions for 20 walks, with areas of interest indicated by symbols (see below). For each walk particular points of interest are denoted by a number both in the text and on the map (where the number appears in a circle). In the text the route instructions are prefixed by a capital letter. We recommend that you read the whole description, including the fact box at the start of each walk, before setting out.

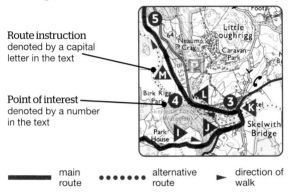

Route instruction
denoted by a capital letter in the text

Point of interest
denoted by a number in the text

━━━━━ main route   •••••••• alternative route   ▶ direction of walk

Key to walk symbols

At the start of each walk there is a series of symbols that indicate particular areas of interest associated with the route.

🐦 Birdlife	🐾 Other wildlife	❀ Wild flowers
☀ Good views	🏰 Historical interest	🌳 Woodland
⛏ Geology	📖 Literature	

SCALE 1:25,000

0	0.25	0.5	0.75	1 kilometre

0		¼		½ mile

Please note the scale for walk maps is 1:25,000 unless otherwise stated
North is always at the top of the page

66 This easy walk around Loweswater makes for a lovely gentle afternoon stroll **99**

Loweswater is in the softer landscape of the Lakes being based on the Skiddaw Slate. The material is more properly described as a shale which breaks down to give a reasonable depth of soil. This means that much of the area not heavily grazed by stock is woodland. Loweswater is in the care of The National Trust, and is little more than a mile (1.6km) long. Much of its shoreline is surrounded by trees and a circumnavigation is an easy and pleasing stroll. Like most of the lakes, Loweswater probably takes its name from an ancient Norse owner; in this case Laghi; 'Laghi's Water'. It is unique in the Lake District in that the flow goes inwards (eastwards) towards the District's centre. It flows, in fact, into Crummock Water before that lake flows outwards to the north as the River Cocker.

A view across Loweswater

Round Loweswater

1

Watergate, Loweswater

Plan your walk

Carlisle
Cockermouth • Penrith
Workington • Keswick
Whitehaven
Windermere
Kendal
Ulverston
Barrow-in-Furness
Lancaster
Heysham

DISTANCE: 4 miles (6.4km)

TIME: 2 hours

START/END: NY121223
From a terraced layby to the northeast of the lake, between the road and the lake

TERRAIN: Easy

MAPS:
OS Explorer OL 4;
OS Landranger 89

Route instructions

A Start the walk from the car park on the road above the lake. Alternatively there is another car park by the telephone box a little further along the road. Walk along the road above the lake in the direction of Loweswater village.

B Leave the road to follow the path beside the lake.

C If the water level in the lake is high you may have to return to the road.

D When a fence blocks the way ahead, go back up to the road and turn right onto it, opposite a pinfold.

E Continue on the road up the hill, and then turn right down a tarmac lane, signposted 'Public Bridleway – Loweswater'.

F After the curves in the road, turn right, through the National Trust car park, and walk along the track across the fields.

1 Viewpoint over the field to the lake.

G At Watergate Farm, pass in front of the buildings, through the gate and along the lakeside path.

2 Tree spotters can note the wide variety of hardwoods grown here. As this is National Trust land there is freedom to wander and identify species or to linger on the shore.

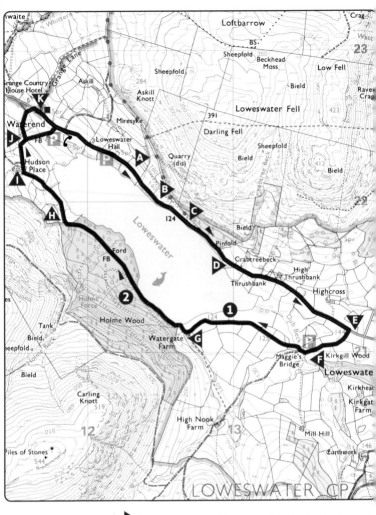

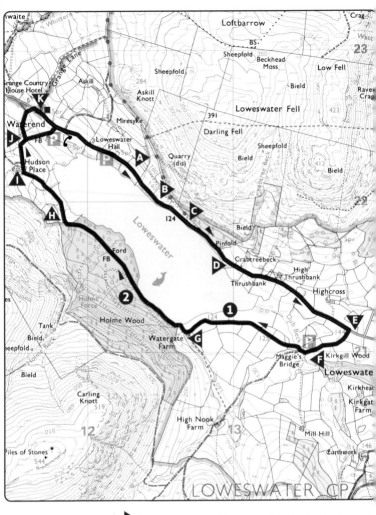 **H** Continue on the path alongside the wall and away from the lake.

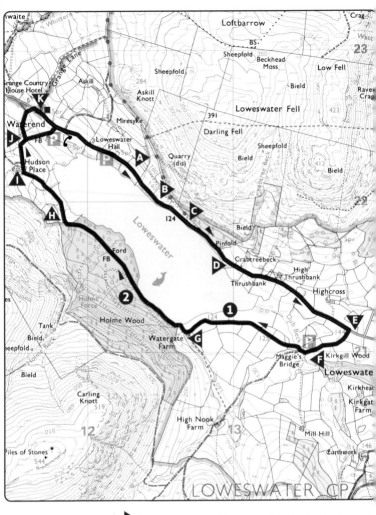 **I** At Hudson Place turn right and go down a 'hollow lane'

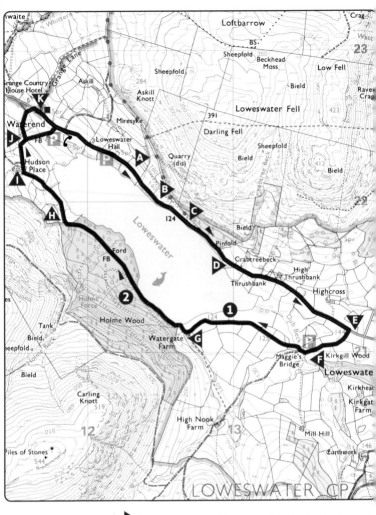 **J** There is a choice of paths here. Either continue straight on, or turn right to cut the corner by going through the gate, down and over a wooden bridge, and up to a gate at the roadside

 K In either case, turn right onto the road and follow it back to the starting point.

Round Loweswater

Holmes Wood, Loweswater

" The lakeside path is flat and easy on the feet making for a pleasant walk for families; children will particularly enjoy going through the rock tunnel "

Many regard the walk round Buttermere as one of the best in the National Park. This lovely lake, which probably takes its name from Buthar, an 11th century Norse chieftan, is set in a craggy tree-clad valley. At its head is Fleetwith Pike towering above Honister Pass, and to the south are the curved ridges of High Crag and High Stile, with their two great hollows and craggy arms which seem to be reaching out to embrace the lake. At the lake foot the steep wall of Red Pike is scored with the slim, silver line of Sour Milk Gill. The lake can be wild when windy, shimmery in the sunshine and sometimes calm and unaccountably dark green. The lakeside path is flat and easy on the feet with plenty of places to stop and picnic. It is a pleasant walk for families, and children will particularly enjoy the surprise when the path goes through a rock tunnel.

Scenic view of Lake Buttermere

Round Buttermere

2

Sour Milk Gill,
Buttermere

Route instructions

A The walk starts at Gatesgarth Farm. If the car park is full it may be possible to park on the Honister road.

B Walk on the track past the farmyard, signposted 'Public Bridleway, Lakeside Path'. Follow it across a field.

C Cross the bridge, go through the gate and turn right.

D Continue on the path beside the lake.

E Turn right through a gate, over a bridge and then over a second, larger bridge.

There is a good view up the lake to Fleetwith Pike.

Look back the way you have walked to see the long line of Sour Milk Gill.

F Follow the track to the tarmac road which passes the Fish Hotel, and then turn right onto the main road beside the Bridge Hotel.

G 50yds (46m) after you join the main road, turn off right onto a track that goes between the farm buildings, signposted 'Public Bridleway, Lakeshore Path'.

H At the fork, turn right through the gate and follow the path downhill, then shortly afterwards bear left through another gate, signposted 'Shoreline Path'.

Plan your walk

DISTANCE: 4 miles (6.4km)

TIME: 2 hours

START/END: NY195149 Gatesgarth

TERRAIN: Easy

MAPS:
OS Explorer OL 4;
OS Landranger 89

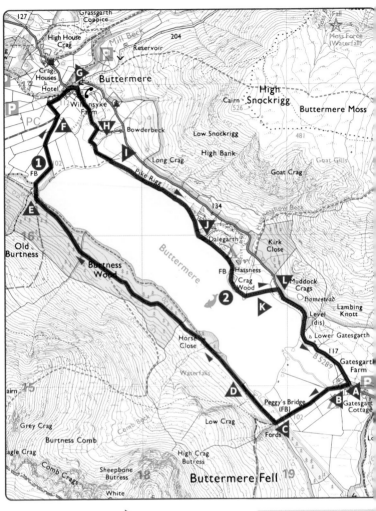

I Follow the lakeshore path.

J The path goes through a rock tunnel.

2 Shingle Point is a classic viewpoint. Opposite is High Crag to the left and High Stile to the right with the views framed by Scots Pines. Fleetwith Pike tower above the lake head.

K Path returns to the road

L Walk on or beside the road, back to the starting point.

Round Buttermere

Fleetwith Pike

> 66 This walk takes you along the west and south shores of this beautiful lake. The outward journey to the start of the walk is by boat 99

Derwent Water is widely regarded as one of the most beautiful lakes in the Lake District. It is now largely under the care of the National Trust but during the mining boom of the 18th century the lake was a highway for barges transporting charcoal and ore. The mines on the western shore have long since closed and the jetties that were used to load and unload are now busy with people enjoying the regular boat services that encircle the lake. The boat service gives walkers an opportunity to walk and picnic on the lakeside paths and to avoid unnecessary road walking. For this route walkers need to consult boat timetables to take the boat to Hawse End landing, and be picked up at Lodore (anti-clockwise service).

Timetables are available on-line www.keswick-launch.co.uk or from information centres.

Derwent Water West Shore

Derwent Water

Route instructions

A Disembark at Hawse End and follow the lakeshore footpath to your left.

B Path leaves shore temporarily through stile and along field edge.

C At end of field go through the gate then turn sharp left and follow this path back to the lakeshore. Follow this around the headland.

1 The view over the lake includes St Herbert's, the nearest island. This is said to be where the saint had his hermitage. Legend has it that he was such a close friend of St Cuthbert of Lindisfarne that they vowed they would die on the same day, which they did in AD687.

The west shore of the lake is in the softer area of the Skiddaw Slates, but opposite there is a notable contrast with the hard and craggy rock of the Borrowdale Volcanics which weathers less easily and more irregularly. From here the opposite shore includes a view of Walla Crag, a popular fell with fine views of Keswick from the 1243ft (379m) summit.

A little further on you pass a large sculpture of a pair of cupped hands carved in oak to commemorate the centenary of the purchase of Brandelhow Park, the first piece of land in the Lake District to be acquired by the National Trust.

Plan your walk

DISTANCE: 3 miles (4.8km)

TIME: 1½ hours

START/END: NY250213 Hawse End landing (you need to get a boat to it!)

TERRAIN: Easy

MAPS:
OS Explorer OL 4;
OS Landranger 89

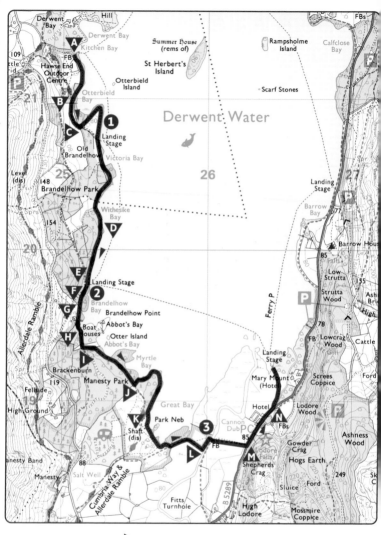

D Keep to the lakeshore path.

E At the landing stage, bear right and join a track.

F Shortly afterwards ignore track to right, and return to the shore. Follow this path around the spoil heaps and through a gate.

2 On the eastern slope of Cat Bells are the disused workings and waste heaps from former lead mines.

Derwent Water
West Shore

Mining began here in ancient times when the ore was worked by hand. Work continued like that for centuries, until in 1848 the Keswick Mining Company put in a 30ft (9.2m) water wheel at the Brandley mine. Since then upgrades to production continued, and more powerful engines were installed but the workings eventually became uneconomic and production ceased in the 1890s.

G Go between a cottage and a boathouse and through a gate.

H At a fork, keep right (left is a private drive).

I At the next fork, by a cottage, go left and along a fence back to the lakeshore.

J Go over the stile in the wall, and then bear left and follow lakeshore path around headland.

K Join another path, but bear left, keeping to the lakeshore.

L Follow the path over walkways and the footbridge over the river.

3 This is a good view over the entire length of the lake with Skiddaw prominent at the lake head. As you turn to look at the path ahead the crag you can see is Shepherd's Crag which is very popular with climbers due to easy access and the varied grades of available ascents.

M 325yds (300m) after the bridge, the path comes to the main road, turn left.

N After passing the Lodore Hotel, take the path on the left leading to the landing stage.

Descending the path from Cat Bells

> **66** This walk combines several notable attractions of the once remote, but now popular, hanging valley of Watendlath, such as the 90ft (27.4m) Lodore Falls and picturesque Ashness Bridge **99**

The awe inspiring view of the thunderous falls at Lodore has been considered an essential part of any tourist's visit to this area since Victorian times. The Lakeland poet Robert Southey wrote his famous onomatopoeic poem 'The Cataract of Lodore' in 1820 to describe the cascading descent of Watlendlath Beck over the edge into Borrowdale. Further up the valley Ashness Bridge, with the picturesque view of the upper part of Derwent Water beyond, is one of the most photographed and painted scenes in Britain although the neighbouring viewpoint, 'Surprise View', is more dramatic. Watendlath was also made popular by the Keswick author Hugh Walpole and his bestselling 1931 novel, Judith Paris, which was set in the hamlet at the head of the valley. Parking can often be a problem around Borrowdale and it is suggested that the walk should start at Lodore after a bus ride there, or after a trip by boat on Derwent Water to the Lodore landing stage. The walk finishes at Ashness Gate where it is also possible to get a boat or bus back. However, at quiet times it should be possible to park in the car park by the lakeshore halfway between Lodore and Ashness Gate (Kettlewell car park). From here you can walk to and from the start and finish. The walk described is from Lodore landing.

Lodore, Watendlath & Ashness

Lodore Falls

Route instructions

A From the boat landing, walk up to the road and turn right. Pass the Lodore Hotel and then turn sharp left around the back of the buildings, following the sign 'To the falls'. Cross the footbridge, bear right into the wood and continue to the viewpoint at **1**.

1 After heavy rain the Lodore Falls are impressive. The largest drop is 90ft (27.4m).

B From the viewpoint, continue upwards on the path which goes left away from the beck. After 160yds (150m) turn sharp right on to a smaller path, which heads upwards and back towards the beck. The going here is difficult as you pass

between boulders and around fallen trees. Caution will be needed if wet.

2 Good views on ascent.

C After another ½ mile (800m), bear left at a fork in the path and continue up and over a stile.

D Continue on the path which follows the course of the beck upstream, until you join a larger track just before a gate in the wall. Go through the gate and turn sharp right. Go down and cross the footbridge and turn left onto a path beside the beck, for 1¼ miles (2km).

E When you reach Watendlath cross the river

Plan your walk

DISTANCE: 4½ miles (7.2km)

TIME: 2¼ hours

START/END: NY264192 Lordore Hotel in the hamlet of Lordore

TERRAIN: Moderate; some wet areas and rough sections

MAPS:
OS Explorer OL 4;
OS Landranger 89

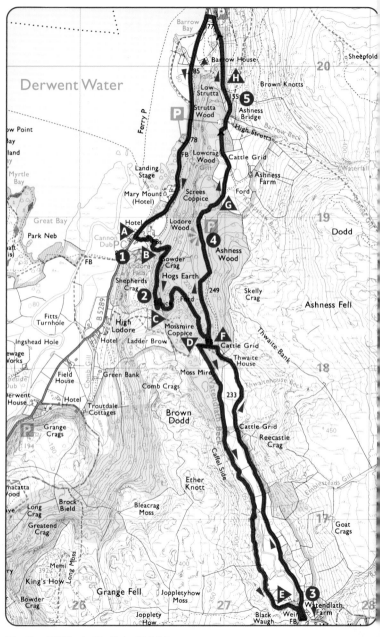

Lodore, Watendlath & Ashness

by the packhorse bridge.
You now have a choice of
route. If the road is not too
busy you could continue by
turning left along the road
and following it all the way
down to **4** ('Surprise
View'). Otherwise retrace
your steps along the path
by the beck to the
footbridge at **D** as
described below.

3 Watendlath is a tiny
hamlet of scattered farm
buildings and a tea room, all
under the care of the
National Trust. Watendlath
Tarn is stocked with both
brown trout and rainbow
trout and is very popular
with anglers.

F Recross the footbridge,
go up and turn left through
the gate, and then follow
the track straight on and up
to join the tarmac road. Turn
left and after 325yds (300m)
arrive at **4**.

4 'Surprise View' is a
stunning tree-framed
eagle's eye view over
Derwent Water to the north-
western fells. On a clear
day it is possible to see
Bassenthwaite Lake in the
distance.

G Continue down the road
to the bridge at **5**.

5 Ashness Bridge is a
traditional stone-built
packhorse bridge and a
popular site for
photography, picnics and
paddling. The famous view
includes Borrowdale and
across Derwent Water to
Keswick and Skiddaw.

H Continue down the road
until you reach the junction
with the main road. Cross
over to the boat landing.
Alternatively, to return to
the Kettlewell car park,
turn sharp left and follow
the main road and lakeside
path back to the car park.

River Derwent

> ❝ Although this is a fairly short walk, you do need to have a certain level of fitness as there are some fairly steep climbs with rough terrain ❞

This is a superb walk for a fine day as it offers some spectacular alpine views. High Rigg is a modest fell between the A591 road from Thirlmere to Keswick and the minor road up St John's in the Vale. There is the tiny isolated church of St John at one end and a glorious pine clad crag at the other; an airy rocky ridge with many superb prospects in between. The walk is for people who are fit, even though it is only four and a half miles (7.2km) there is a steep ascent of 700ft (213.3m) and some rough terrain. Strong and grippy footwear is essential. It is best to treat this walk as a whole day out, for there are many idyllic picnic and loitering spots. The walk starts fairly easily and pleasantly along the riverside. The more strenuous parts are in the middle and towards the end of the route.

High Rigg

View of Low Rigg and High Rigg

DISTANCE: 4½ miles (7.2km)

TIME: 2¼ hours

START/END: NY317195 Water Authority's car park ¼ mile north of Stanah, Thirlmere on the St John's (Threlkeld) road

TERRAIN: Strenuous

MAPS:
OS Explorer OL 4;
OS Landranger 90

Route instructions

▶ Start at the United Utilities car park and picnic area 550yds (500m) north of Stanah, Thirlmere on the B5322 St John's in the Vale (Threlkeld) road. Walk out of the car park towards the picnic area, but turn left onto the old road which takes you up to the main Keswick road. Turn right along the verge and, immediately after crossing the bridge, turn right over the stile onto the footpath.

▶ Shortly afterwards ignore a faint path to the right and a little further keep straight on at a junction on a narrow but good path parallel with the river.

1 This is a delightful path on a wooded terrace with a good view of the river.

▶ The path nears the river by some large boulders, then bears away from it to follow a wall to the left.

▶ After a stile and a gate, climb left to follow the path above the farm buildings and tearoom.

▶ Continue on this path, with the wall on your right, until you reach the ruined building at Sosgill. Divert right at this point and walk across the bridge.

2 Sosgill Bridge, a stone arched bridge with a fine view of Blencathra (Saddleback).

▶ From the bridge, follow

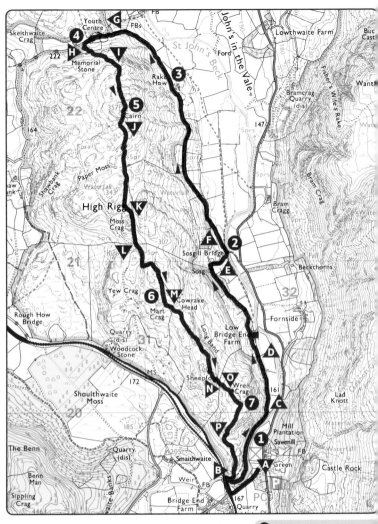

the faint path across the field to the gate, and turn right and rejoin the main path.

3 Rake How, a ruined farm.

G Join the tarmac road and turn left.

4 St John's Church. The isolated situation may seem odd, but the road here was once well used. The first written reference to the church was in 1554, but the site predates that as it was built on the site of an earlier church. The existing

High Rigg

building dates from 1845. The atmosphere inside is homely and friendly. Nearby is buried St John's best known personality, John Richardson (1817–1866) the talented dialect poet who helped to build the church.

J Go on past the church and then immediately after the youth centre turn left onto a path. Follow it uphill and through a kissing gate.

K Continue upwards on a grassy path to the ridge.

5 Summit cairn. Spectacular views over to Blencathra (Saddleback) 2847ft/867.7m) to the right; Skiddaw (3054ft/930.8m) to the left and to the far left Grisedale Pike, Causey Pike and Bassenthwaite Lake.

L From the cairn follow the path which goes downhill and across to a wall corner. This is open fell and you can make detours to take in the views.

L The path continues to the right of the wall and reaches a boggy area. The worst of this can be avoided by taking a sweep to the right and returning leftwards under the face of a small crag.

L Follow the wall down and over a stile, then bear left up a small path to regain the ridge.

M Pass a small tarn and follow a fence for a further 220yds (200m), then turn left over a stile and follow this path along the ridge.

6 Views. Helvellyn is ahead. The 3113ft (948.8m) summit is almost obscured by Whiteside and Low Man. Thirlmere is seen between the impressive wooded jaws of Great How and Raven Crag.

N To get off the ridge with as little difficulty as possible, aim for a gap in the wall ahead, bearing left off the ridge to follow the path down and through the gap.

O Follow the path ahead onto the summit of Wren Crag, just above the pine trees.

7 Exciting views here framed in some beautifully sculpted Scots Pines.

P Descend steeply on the path through the woods, and rejoin the outward route at **B**. Turn right at the path junction, go over the stile and retrace your steps back to the car park.

66 This walk, which follows the course of Stonethwaite Beck offers some lovely views up the valley to the impressive mass of Eagle Crag **99**

Stonethwaite is a tiny settlement which has given its name to a narrow side-valley off Borrowdale. Ancient pack pony routes run from this valley to Grasmere via Greenup, and to Langdale via Stake Pass. The route forks below the dominating hulk of Eagle Crag. Stonethwaite is well named ('thwaite' means a place, clearing or settlement), therefore literally this is a place of stones. There are millions of them, brought down by the pounding fury of the often storm-swollen Langstrath Beck and Greenup Gill, to form a stone-filled river bed.

The walk starts at Rosthwaite, where car parking is limited. Alternatively it may be possible to park at **C** (Stonethwaite) or on the approach road. From the small National Trust car park in Rosthwaite, turn right and then left and follow the narrow road through the village.

Stonethwaite

River Derwent

Route instructions

A The walk starts at Rosthwaite, where car parking is limited. Alternatively it may be possible to park at **C** (Stonethwaite) or on the approach road.

From the small National Trust car park in Rosthwaite, turn right and then left and follow the narrow road through the village.

B After 160yds (150m), turn right off the road and then shortly afterwards turn left onto a footpath across the fields, signposted to Longthwaite Youth Hostel.

C After passing the houses at Peat Howe, go straight on at the junction. Follow

this road up to the main road, then go straight across and continue on past the school to Stonethwaite village.

D Turn left at the telephone box in the village onto a track.

E Follow the track down to cross the bridge and at the T junction, turn right and follow the path beside the river.

1 Good view up the valley towards the impressive mass of Eagle Crag.

2 The path passes Galleny Force, where there are several small waterfalls and pools often known as the 'Fairy Glen'.

Plan your walk

DISTANCE: 4 miles (6.4km)

TIME: 2 hours

START/END: NY257148 Rosthwaite

TERRAIN: Easy; some rough ground

MAPS:
OS Explorer OL 4;
OS Landranger 89

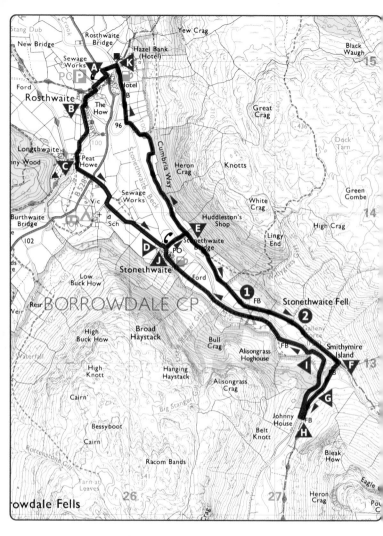

F Pass the sheep pens and then turn right to cross the footbridge.

G Wet ground can be avoided with care. Continue on until you come to a second footbridge.

H Cross the footbridge and turn right on to the track.

I At the bottom of the hill, where the main track bears left, go to the right of a sheepfold and through a gate onto the riverside path.

Stonethwaite

which you follow across the fields and back into Stonethwaite.

 At the telephone box turn right and retrace the outward route over the bridge to **E**. This time, turn left at the T junction, and follow the path downstream.

 After about ¾ mile (just over 1km) on this path, turn left over the stone bridge and left again at the main road. After 110yds (100m) turn right into the village and arrive back at the car park.

Eagle Crag

> 66 Short walk with a steep climb via Dob Gill.
> The route then takes you along a forest track
> through the woods and onto a viewpoint
> over Thirlmere and Helvellyn 99

This walk overlooks a glacial valley within which the reservoir of Thirlmere was created in the 19th century to satisfy the demand for water from Manchester during the Industrial Revolution. Before the flooding of the valley there were two small tarns, Leathes Water and Wythburn Water. A stream connecting the tarns was spanned by a stone bridge. By 1894 Manchester Corporation had acquired the valley and dammed the lake to raise it by 50ft (15.2m), and the reservoir of Thirlmere was created, drowning the hamlets of Wythburn and Armboth. Only the higher-level chapel of Wythburn, to the east of the newly created road, now the A591, remains. An important packhorse route once ran from Wythburn in the valley bottom (then known locally as 'the city') to Watendlath and Borrowdale. This walk starts on the packhorse route to go uphill to Harrop Tarn, then returns through the forest.

The walk starts at a small car park on the western minor road. Join this road at its junction with the A591 (Ambleside to Keswick road), south of the lake. Follow this road for a mile (1.6km). The car park is on a bank to the left.

Harrop Tarn

Thirlmere from Bank Crags

Route instructions

A The walk starts at the 'Dobgill' car park which is on the minor road along the west side of Thirlmere. Turn left off the A591 Ambleside to Keswick road at the junction just south of the head of the lake, and the car park is almost a mile (1.5km) along the minor road on the left. Leave the car park, turn right onto the road and walk south along it.

B After crossing Dob Gill, ignore the public bridleway going uphill and continue along the road for another 220yds (200m) before turning right through a gate. Don't follow the public bridleway ahead, but turn right again over a stile and follow the path up to **1**.

1 The crag has a viewpoint of the fell of Helvellyn on the other side of Thirlmere, although the summit is too far back to be seen.

C Continue up the path to join the bridleway and follow this steeply uphill.

D Go over the stile and continue up through the woods, cross the tarn outlet by a footbridge and walk on beside the tarn, following the footpath arrows.

2 Viewpoint over Harrop Tarn. This is a peaceful tarn, fringed by conifers. A gradual silting of the tarn means it is shallow and thick with reeds at the

Plan your walk

DISTANCE: 2 miles (3.2km)

TIME: 1 hour

START/END: NY315140 Small car park on a minor road that runs along the southern and western edge of Thirlmere, just off the A591

TERRAIN: Moderate; wet areas

MAPS: OS Explorer OL 4; OS Landranger 90

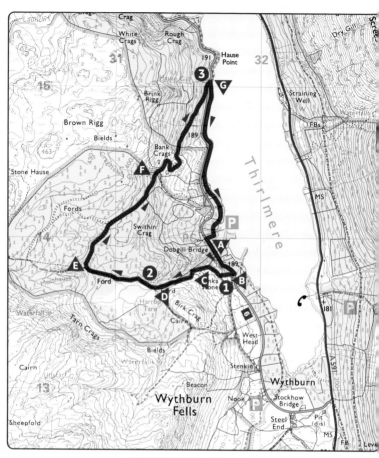

edges. At the eastern edge of the tarn Dob Gill emerges to fall in a series of waterfalls into Thirlmere.

E Ignore the bridleway going straight on and which climbs up and over to Watendlath, and instead turn right here onto a good forest track and follow this through the woods.

F When you come to a gate at the edge of the woods,

go through it and follow the track round the zig-zags and down to the road.

G Turn sharp right onto the road and follow this back to the starting point. Alternatively you can follow a waymarked path through the woods below the road.

3 There is a good viewpoint for Thirlmere and Helvellyn just as you join the road.

Harrop Tarn

Thirlmere from Great How

> ❝ This short walk is particularly rewarding after heavy rain when the waters of Aira Beck look extremely impressive as they plummet over the 80ft (24.4m) waterfall ❞

This could be a walk suitable for a wet day as not only is it short and partly sheltered by attractive woodland but any heavy rainfall on the hills dramatically increases the flow of the Aira Beck as it plummets over the waterfall on its way to Ullswater. Aira Force is one of the most famous and most visited of the Lake District waterfalls and was an inspiration to Wordsworth who described it as 'A powerful brook, which dashes among rocks through a deep glen, hung on every side with a rich and happy intermixture of native wood'.[1]

Stone footbridges span the beck both above and below the falls, allowing for excellent views. Note that the wet rock of the path can be very slippery so suitable footwear is essential and also that dogs are not allowed on the permitted footpaths through the fields during lambing season, and should be on leads in the fields at all other times.

Reference:
[1] Wordsworth 'W. Guide to the English Lakes'. London, 1835.

Aira Force

Route instructions

A A National Trust car park serves the falls and is just to the east of the junction between the A592 (Ullswater shore road) and the A5091 Dockray Road. At the far end of the car park go through the archway and follow the signs to the falls.

B Turn right and go through the gate into the wood.

1 Wordsworth was an enthusiast for 'the intermixture of native wood' and abhorred the introduction of alien species. Here, however, there is an effective mixture of mainly native deciduous trees together with some alien conifers to produce a very pretty woodland along the course of this route. All the area of this walk is in the care of The National Trust.

C Cross two bridges and go up the steps ahead. Bear left and go along a terraced path.

D Go onto the bridge for a view up the falls. Come back along the path for a short distance and then turn left up the steep steps and follow the path across to the upper bridge above the falls.

2 The view upwards from the lower bridge reveals an 80ft (24.4m) fall. The scene is enhanced by the tree and fern growth on the steep banks. The view from the second bridge reveals the

Plan your walk

DISTANCE: 2 miles (3.2km)

TIME: 1 hour

START/END: NY400200 A car park at the base of the Falls to east of the junction of the road from Dockray (A5091) with the Ullswater shore road (A592)

TERRAIN: Moderate; some slippery sections

MAPS:
OS Explorer OL 5;
OS Landranger 90

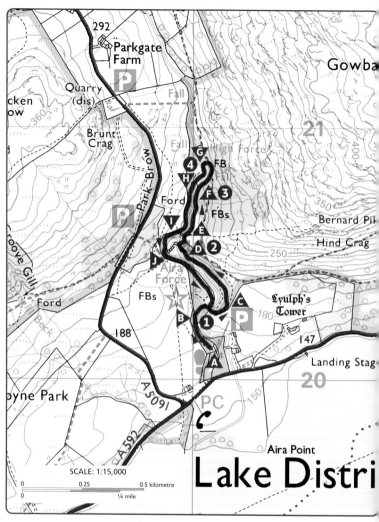

fall dropping to the giddy depths below.

E Retrace your steps for a short distance and then turn left onto a small path which follows the river upstream.

F Cross a small footbridge

and come to a viewpoint of the gorge above.

3 Here the beck flows down through a narrow channel.

G Continue upstream on the path, bearing left at a

Aira Force

junction with a higher path. Shortly afterwards bear left and down to cross the river by a footbridge. Nearby are several places to view the series of cascades.

4 From just above, the upper waterfall of High Force can be viewed. It is less spectacular than Aira Force but is still very pleasant and can be much less crowded.

▶ Descend on the path on the other bank of the river until you reach the upper bridge once again.

▶ At this point there is a choice of routes. You could return by your outward route, but the recommended alternative is to turn right at the upper bridge and follow the path up the steps. This affords more excellent views of Aira Force.

▶ Take the right fork by a seat (ignoring the steps descending to your left), and follow this path, keeping inside the wall. This eventually brings you down to join the outward path. Turn right and retrace your steps to the car park.

Cascading waterfall

66 Pleasant walk up the old mine track to Greenside following Glenridding Beck from the jetty on Ullswater **99**

The extremely productive Greenside lead mines to the west of Glenridding, which were in production from the 18th to the middle of the 20th centuries have left their mark on the landscape of the Glenridding Valley in the form of mine tracks and an old aqueduct. However, considering the size of the operation which was shut down in 1962, not a huge amount is obvious today. The mining company, and subsequently the National Parks Authority, have carried out a fair bit of landscaping work. But if you know what to look out for you will see such buildings as a gunpowder store and a couple of other mining buildings dotted around along the walk route.

Glenridding & Greenside Mine

Gillside

Route instructions

A The walk starts at the Glenridding car park. Go out of the pedestrian exit in the top corner of the car park, past the health centre and turn left onto the road up through the village.

B Bear right at the end of the village, 220yds (200m) beyond the Travellers Rest pub. Follow this road up and past a row of terraced cottages where it becomes a track. This is then followed up the valley to the old mine buildings.

1 The small building on the right was the gunpowder store which was always situated well away from the main workings. Few other buildings remain; two are being used as hostels. Note

the stabilisation work on the surface of the tailing dams.

C Continue on the track through the old mine buildings, up the zigzag and then bear left down to the footbridge over the beck.

D Cross the bridge and turn left down the path.

2 There is a pleasant view to the left. The illusion is given that the walk on this aqueduct is down hill or level. In fact this is not so. Water was collected and taken back to the workings behind.

E After 325yds (300m) leave the line of the old aqueduct and drop to the left on the signed footpath.

DISTANCE: 3½ miles (5.6km)

TIME: 1¾ hours

START/END: NY385169 Glenridding car park

TERRAIN: Easy

MAPS:
OS Explorer OL 5;
OS Landranger 90

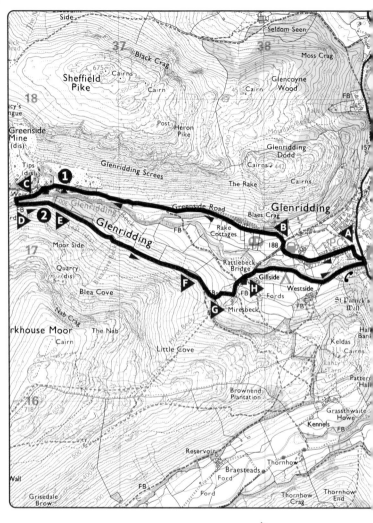

Follow this beside the wall until you come to a stile.

F Go left over the stile and continue down the path.

G Turn left onto the track and follow this down past the farm.

H Just before the bridge over the beck, turn right a follow the riverside path in front of the camp site and on until you reach the ma road. Turn left over the bridge and back into the c park.

Glenridding & Greenside Mine

View towards Glenridding

Greenside sits in a valley east of Helvellyn above the village of Glenridding, and at one time had one of the most profitable lead mines in the north of England. It was in production from the late 18th century to the middle of the 20th century. It was estimated that by 1876 it had produced some 40,000 tons (40,642 tonnes) of smelted lead, and 600,000oz (24,000g) of silver. In 1891 electrical winding gear was introduced. It was the first metal mine in the country to use it. The workings were extremely intensive and went deep into Helvellyn. An electrical locomotive (another first) was also used for drawing material from the productive shafts a mile (1.6km) into the mountain. Originally this work was done by seven horses. Compressed air, for driving the drills, was provided by electricity. By modern standards the generating plant and installations were crude and dangerous, but they were worked with little mishap. Ore was smelted on the site and the furnace flue was carried 1½ miles (2.4km) up the mountain so that lead vapour could condense on the flue sides to be collected for return to the furnace. Water power was provided from the falls of Red Tarn and Keppie Cove Tarn above, the latter was dammed. This dam burst in a great storm in 1927 and a wall of water smashed through the workings and the village causing great damage, but miraculously no loss of life. The remaining sign of this disaster is the promontory east of Glenridding formed from the debris and on which the steamer pier now stands.

Hardly anything remains of the works buildings and all is silent now. The mine was sealed in 1962 after the Atomic Energy Authority conducted seismic tests with conventional explosives deep in the workings. The old 'tailing dams' consisting of vast quantities of waste material were partly covered by the mining company with grass and trees and further work has been carried out by the National Parks Authority.

> **❝** This walk follows the river side, past the dale's little church, and finishes by climbing up alongside the waterfall to an airy viewpoint on top of a precipice. **❞**

Eskdale lacks only a lake but it has everything else. It is a long dale with its head under the highest land in England and its foot in the sea, and it has an incredible variety of landscape types. It would take almost a lifetime to explore it thoroughly. It has a history too. Down this dale came the stone axes roughed out by Neolithic craftsmen. They were then carried to the coastal sandstone for polishing and sharpening. The Romans improved the Anglo Saxon road and built a fort on one of the dale's spectacular vantage points, at Hardknott, and another to guard their port at the dale's foot at Ravenglass. Then followed the Viking settlements. After the Norman conquest the monks of Furness Abbey claimed much of the valley, managing the deer herds and probably opening the first iron mines here which produced high quality ore until the 19th century. The middle and lower reaches of the dale are walled by crags of granite, much of it coloured pink by the iron content. In one great wooded ravine in its southern side there flows a beautiful waterfall, known as both Dalegarth Falls and Stanley Ghyll Force.

Eskdale Ramble & Dalegarth Waterfalls

'River Irt' on Ravenglass railway

Route instructions

A There are two possible starting points. One is in the car park beside the terminus of the narrow-gauge railway ('La'al Ratty') at Dalegarth Station. Turn right down the main road and then turn left by the small war memorial. Alternatively, start from the Trough House Bridge car park which is down the road going to Dalegarth Hall. In this case turn back right out of the car park and cross the bridge.

B From these starting points you approach a bend in the road from opposite directions. In both cases turn east off the road onto a footpath, signposted 'St. Catherine's Church'.

1 A Chapel was established in Eskdale as long ago as the 12th century. In the 15th century the chapel was promoted to a parish church. This upgrading followed a successful petition to the Pope which complained about the hardships experienced in travelling to St. Bees for burials and baptisms. The church was rebuilt in 1881. In the churchyard there are two interesting gravestones to two notable huntsmen, Tommy Dobson and Willy Porter.

C On leaving the church, follow the path to the left (east), beside the river.

Plan your walk

Carlisle
Cockermouth Penrith
Workington Keswick
Whitehaven
Windermere
Kendal
Ulverston
Barrow-in-Furness
Lancaster
Heysham

DISTANCE: 4 miles (6.4km)

TIME: 2 hours

START/END: NY173007 Dalegarth station car park or a car park on the Dalegarth road

TERRAIN: Moderate; some rough sections

MAPS:
OS Explorer OL 6;
OS Landranger 96

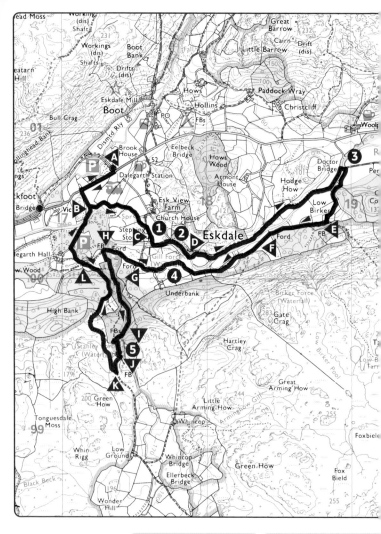

2 There are some beautiful clear pools in the river bed. Look for the restored mine bridge. This is a wooden footbridge built on the top of girders that used to carry the tramway which transported the ore. The bridge was rebuilt in 1990 memory of Geoffrey Berry, former secretary of the Friends of the Lake Distric

D Don't cross this footbridge but continue on the riverside path for

Eskdale Ramble & Dalegarth Waterfalls

another 1km until you reach Doctor Bridge. Cross this bridge and turn right onto the track signposted 'Public Bridleway: Dalegarth'.

3 Doctor Bridge is an attractive arch bridge made of local stone.

E Just above Low Birker Farm, bear right onto a clear track between walls.

F The track continues parallel with the river, passing an attractive little tarn with a seat.

4 Signs of mining activity around include very red earth, and waste tips.

G At the junction continue straight on, across a shallow ford and then to a footbridge.

H Cross the footbridge but don't go through the gate. Instead turn left and follow the path up through the woods beside the river.

I Cross two bridges and then go onto a third, which is the viewpoint bridge. The main path turns here, but the fit and agile might scramble with care up the far bank for more views of the falls, though they must then return to the bridge. Retrace your route for a short way, then go up the steep steps. Turn left at a T junction, over a small footbridge and up to another viewpoint.

5 Those with no head for heights will have to be content with standing back and children should be closely controlled. There is a sheer drop into the gill at this point, and there is a grand view northwards over the Eskdale valley, which is framed by trees.

J Leave this viewpoint and continue up the path to a stile over the fence, and shortly afterwards you arrive at a good track.

K Turn right and follow the track down.

L At the crossroads carry straight on, then go past the entrance to Dalegarth Hall and back to either starting point.

Eskdale

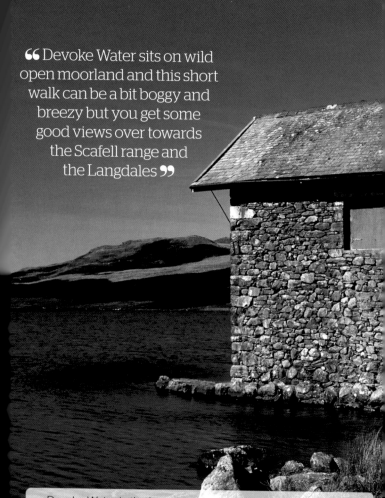

66 Devoke Water sits on wild open moorland and this short walk can be a bit boggy and breezy but you get some good views over towards the Scafell range and the Langdales **99**

Devoke Water is the largest and one of the highest tarns in the Lake District, similar in size to Brotherswater. It is a mountain tarn open to the sky, lashed by Atlantic winds, its mood responds quickly to the changing weather. It has an untamed appeal and this walk around the tarn is a breezy one on rather sketchy paths but with the opportunity, for the adventurous, to pioneer their own routes. There are, however, boggy areas, the worst of which can be avoided with care. It is worth remembering that heather will not flourish on very wet ground.

Scenic view of Devoke Water

Devoke Water

Route instructions

A Park your car by the roadside by the minor road opposite the track for Devoke Water. The walk starts here and you follow the track across to the edge of Devoke Water.

B Continue on the track which bears left around the tarn. Continue straight on, following a smaller path around the tarn, when the track goes right to a boat house at Washfold Point.

1 Viewpoint across the tarn to Water Crag and Rough Crag on the north side.

2 Viewpoint with the Scafell range, Bowfell, and Langdale fells in background.

C As the path passes the western end of the tarn, cut off to the right, continuing around the tarn.

3 At a cairn on slightly higher ground, there is a viewpoint west towards the sea and east over the lake and the fells above Eskdale and Dunnerdale.

D Cross the tarn outlet with care. The route beyond is fairly pathless. Head for higher ground on the lower slopes of Water Crag as you continue around the tarn.

E The boggy areas here are not usually too soft.

F Complete the circuit of the tarn by rejoining the outward track, and retrace your steps back to the starting point.

Plan your walk

DISTANCE: 3 miles (4.8km)

TIME: 1½ hours

START/END: SD170977 Roadside parking on the minor road opposite the track for Devoke Water

TERRAIN: Moderate; wet

MAPS:
OS Explorer OL 6;
OS Landranger 96

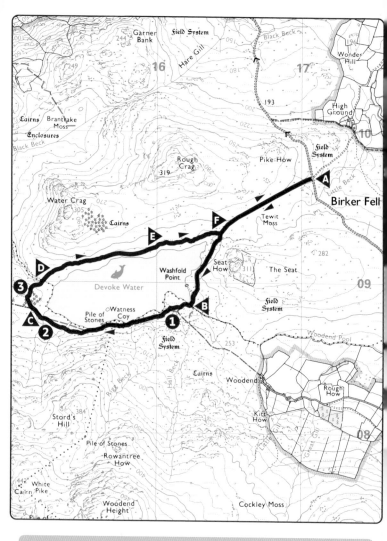

Archaeological evidence, and examination of pollen types found deep in the mud and peat, has shown that in prehistoric times the landscape around Devoke Water was forest, and that there was very extensive human settlement by Neolithic farmers or hunters. There are also many burial mounds and hut circles in the district. Since then, climatic change, and the hand of man has reduced the area to wild open moorland.

Devoke Water

Shore of Devoke Water

> **Lovely 5 mile (8km) walk which takes you from Ulpha up to Frith Hall, where you get some lovely views over Dunnerdale, then on via Beckfoot and back along the valley side of the River Duddon**

The River Duddon is a delight throughout its route. Two roads, either side of the Duddon's lower reaches join at Ulpha (Scandinavian 'ulf-hauga' meaning 'wolf hill'). On whichever road you travel your eyes are drawn to a ruined 'castle' on the hill between. This is Frith Hall, high on the ancient roadway. It is not a castle, but a former hunting lodge for the Ulpha deer park owned by the Huddleston family. At the end of the 16th century it became an Inn and in the 18th century it gained a reputation as being England's 'Gretna Green'. In 1730 seventeen marriages were recorded. In 1736 a guest met a mysterious end, possibly murdered. It is said that his ghost haunts the place.

Lower Duddon & Frith Hall

Bowfell at dawn

Route instructions

A The walk starts south of Ulpha Bridge. A parking space can usually be found by the roadside. Walk up the road to the bridge.

B Cross the bridge and turn left along the road.

C Just after the second bridge on this road, you pass the former mill buildings on your right. Continue on up the steep hill.

1 Much use was made of the running water in these valleys. Here at one time timber from the surrounding coppice woods, was turned to provide bobbins for the Lancashire textile industry.

D As the road levels out and bends to the right, go

left through a gate onto the footpath signposted 'Bleabeck Bridge'.

E Join the track and bear right, through the gate and over the bridge, and on up to pass the ruin.

2 Frith Hall ruin. Good views from a very 'atmospheric' prospect.

F Continue on the track into the woods. This is a pleasant route which then takes you down to the road.

G Turn left and follow the road down.

H Turn sharp left down the track (signposted 'Beckfoot'), and go over a bridge towards the houses.

Plan your walk

DISTANCE: 5 miles (8km)

TIME: 2½ hours

START/END: SD196930 Roadside parking just south of Ulpha Bridge

TERRAIN: Moderate

MAPS: OS Explorer OL 6; OS Landranger 96

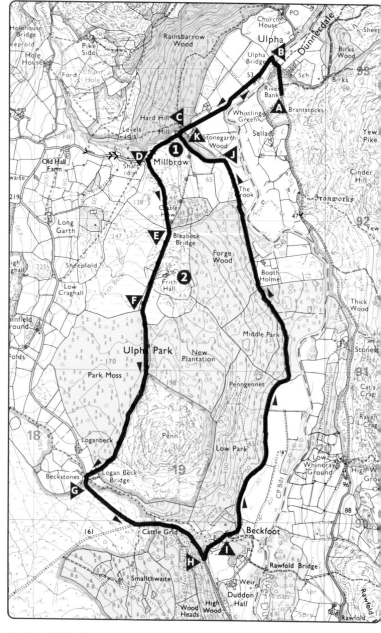

Lower Duddon & Frith Hall

Go over a second bridge, through the farmyard. Ignore a footpath going off to the right and continue down a track through the trees. It then climbs gradually through the woods.

The track curves left.

Come to the road, turn right and retrace your outward route to the starting point.

Dunnerdale

> **66** This walk, although it takes a little more effort than some, is more than worth it for the stunning views when you reach its highest point **99**

There is some steep ground on this route so sandals, wellington boots or smooth-soled shoes should not be worn. Remember that steep grass can be as treacherous as rock. Old mine shafts are another hazard for those whose curiosity may lure them from the path; though the more dangerous ones are fenced. Children and dogs should be kept carefully controlled. Lone walkers should take the precaution of leaving route details with someone at 'base'. Although this walk has these disadvantages the rewards are great. It starts by the waterfall, which is very spectacular after rain and goes via ancient copper mines. After making the ascent to the walk's highest point any breath left could be taken away by the awesome view over Langdale.

Tilberthwaite & Little Langdale

Packhorse bridge, River Brathay

Plan your walk

DISTANCE: 4 miles (6.4km)

TIME: 2 hours

START/END: NY305010 Old quarry parking area at the foot of Tilberthwaite Gill, which is reached by a minor road off the Coniston to Ambleside road

TERRAIN: Moderate; some very steep, rough, wet sections

MAPS: OS Explorer OL 7; OS Landranger 90

Route instructions

Park in the old quarry parking area at the foot of Tilberthwaite Gill, which is reached by a minor road off the Coniston to Ambleside road. From Coniston it is the first turning to the north. From Ambleside it is the second turning on the right after passing the little roadside tarn (Yew Tree Tarn). Climb the steps from the car park and follow the path on the left hand side of Tilberthwaite Gill, following the Gill's course at a higher level.

Bear right, then follow the rough path and steps down to the footbridge across the Gill.

Viewpoint. The fall here is not great but the volume of water is often very considerable. The upper falls cannot be reached. Earlier last century more bridges and catwalks were in position above this viewpoint bridge but they have been swept away by major floods which have torn down the unstable walls of the ravine.

Cross the footbridge and follow the steps and footpath steeply upwards.

The path crosses a fence at a kissing gate and joins the old miners' track. Go left up the path, which runs very close to the ravine with the water cascading down below. Take care as there is a very steep drop on the left.

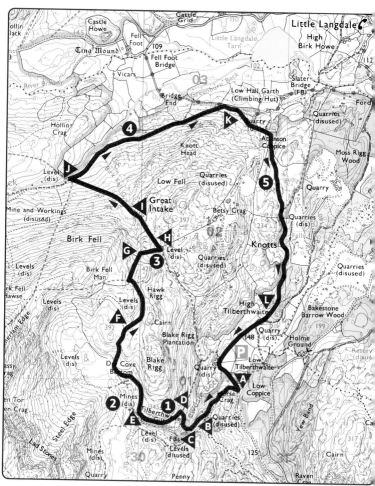

E At the top of the Gill ravine go right on the old miners' track.

2 Everywhere there are signs of copper mine workings. There is some evidence that copper was mined here in Roman times, though inevitably many of the signs of old workings have been destroyed by more recent activity. The last major efforts in this area, including the driving of a 3000ft level (914m), and the sinking of a 390ft shaft (120m), occurred in 1850, but extraction proved too costly and the main production became concentrated in the Coniston Copper Mines to the south-west, and at Greenburn to the north.

Tilberthwaite & Little Langdale

F At this point, near the old mine workings and stonework , where the track bears left for a steep ascent of Wetherlam, go right and upwards on a less distinct path, past further old mine workings. Beware of the collapsed and dangerous mineshaft.

G At the top of this saddle, follow a fairly indistinct path to the right of a fence, descending to a wall.

H Just before reaching the wall, cross the fence by a stile and then cut across to a high step stile over the wall. Cross the stile on to the north side of the wall.

3 There are many fine views of Langdale Pikes but surely none to cap this! In the foreground there is a tumble of crags and between Blake Rigg and Lingmoor, Blea Tarn can be seen. It is surely one of the best mountain prospects in Britain.

I Follow the indistinct path on the north side of the wall, passing a second high step stile half way down.

J Join the miners' track and go right.

4 Enjoy further marvellous views over to Langdale Pikes. Here the foreground is a rocky chaos, a turmoil of craggy shapes, adding more drama. Forward is Little Langdale Tarn. The road over Wrynose begins below in Little Langdale. The modern road follows the old Roman road (the 'Xth iter') over the pass, linking the forts at Ambleside and Hardknott and on to Ravenglass. Its route is not traceable until it reaches the farm of Fell Foot below, but from there onwards it is to the north, the far side, of the present road.

K At the track junction, walk upwards to the right and follow the quarry track straight onwards (detours lead to quarries).

5 Extensive quarrying to the right. The quarrying boom followed the copper mining. A detour to look at the slate might be of interest. The colour varies in each locality. The material was formed from volcanic dust laid down under water and the ripple marks can sometimes be seen. The slate is hard and takes a good polish. In the boom in the 19th century records show that a quarryman was paid a guinea (£1.05) for working a six day week.

L At the end of the track, go through a farm, closing the gates behind you, and continue on the surfaced lane to the starting point.

> **"** Glorious views of the Old Man of Coniston range and, away to the north, you can also see the Helvellyn range from a lovely vantage point above the peaceful lakeside **"**

It is not generally known that there is pedestrian access either by right of way or on public access land, to most of the western shore of Coniston Water. This reveals views unknown to the general tourist, away from traffic noise and bustle. Fast boats are not present on Coniston Water as there is a ten miles (16km) per hour speed limit. This makes it more attractive than Windermere for those who look for serenity. This is an away-from-it-all walk on common land with excellent views, finishing on a lake shore path.

Torver Back Common & Coniston Water Shore

The summit of Coniston Old Man

Route instructions

A The walk starts from the A5084 Torver to Ulverston road 1 mile (1.5km) south of Torver, at Beckstones. There is a layby parking area here opposite a large garage. Walk up through a gate and around to the left of the tarn. Continue up the path with the wall on your left.

B At the wall corner you should see the next tarn ahead. Take the path up the hill to the right of it.

1 Viewpoint above the tarn. Excellent view of Coniston Old Man range and a stretch of the lake. All this is common land. Many years ago this would have been wooded, but the trees have been cleared and the land grazed by sheep. Now most of the land is covered with bracken which spreads rapidly in deep-soiled open land and is almost impossible to eradicate. The grazing area is now very limited. Only a few trees survive here as seedlings are soon eaten by sheep. There are a few mountain ash (rowan).

C Looking up the lake from the viewpoint a path will be seen descending to the outflow of the tarn. Take this path past the tarn, over a small hill and down to a stream to join another path. Follow this down for a short distance and then bear left, up beside another stream and across to **2**.

Carlisle

Cockermouth   Penrith
Workington   Keswick
Whitehaven

Windermere

Kendal

Barrow-in-Furness   Ulverston

Lancaster
Heysham

DISTANCE: 3½ miles (5.6km)

TIME: 1¾ hours

START/END: SD286930 Layby parking area opposite a large garage on the Coniston to Ulverston road, one mile south of Torver

TERRAIN: Moderate; some wet sections

MAPS:
OS Explorer OL 6;
OS Landranger 96

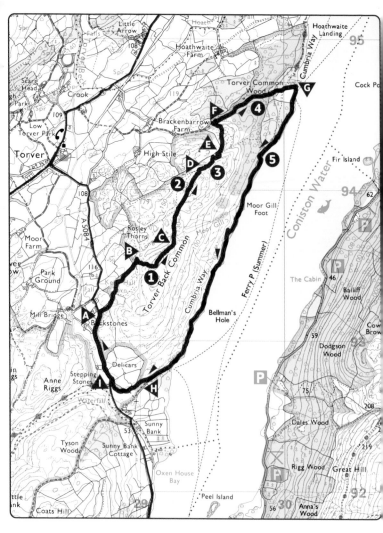

2 This viewpoint gives a perfect view of the Old Man range and there is a small natural stone seat facing it. The view over the lake goes right to the head, and away to the north is the Helvellyn range.

D Continue on this path, dropping into another valley with a wall beyond, and go through the juniper bushes.

3 Junipers are getting scarcer in many parts of the country but they still survive

Torver Back Common & Coniston Water Shore

in the Lake District. Juniper is our only native cypress. Note the varied shapes of the shrubs here; some are quite old. Chew the berries, whether green or ripe, and you will find out how gin gets its flavour. The berries have long been valued in medicine.

E At the point where the wall curves away from the valley, cross the stream and go up the bank opposite to follow the wall round. A short distance afterwards bear off down across the common to the right and join a path.

F When this path joins a larger path just in front of another wall, turn right onto the larger path and descend into the woods.

4 The path goes through woodland which was once coppiced, that is cut every 12 years or so, and new growth allowed to come from the 'stools' (stumps). Formerly these woods were used to supply charcoal for the iron furnaces; mainly oak, alder and birch.

G This path eventually meets the lakeshore just after it crosses another path. At the lake turn right and follow 'The Cumbria Way' along the lakeshore.

5 There are several good viewpoints along the shore with two things in particular to look for along the shoreline. Clinker can still be seen where 'bloomeries', small 'do-it-yourself' smelting operations were carried out here in ancient times. Ore was brought by boat to points where charcoal was readily available. In boggy areas there are insect-eating plants; the butterwort, and the sundew. They are small plants, easily missed, but once identified can be observed in many places.

H Just after the landing stage the path bears to the right, leaving the lakeshore and climbs beside the wall. Just before a wall junction the path bears right away from the wall and climbs across the common to a gate.

I Shortly after going through the gate, you arrive at the main road. Turn right up the road and follow it back to the starting point.

> **This is quite a strenuous walk over fairly rugged terrain, but the views along the route are spectacular**

Holme Fell is a craggy fell wedged between the northern spur of the Coniston Old Man range, and the hills around Tarn Hows. Although modest in height, it is an exciting summit, rough, humpy and scrubby, with a thrilling view over to Langdale, to Helvellyn and Fairfield and High Street. Particularly close at hand is the great bulk of Wetherlam. There is a pleasant feeling of wildness and isolation and possibly an exaggerated sense of achievement in the adventurous final scramble up to Ivy Crag.

Obviously strong footwear is required for this walk, which should not be attempted in bad weather.

Low Water and Wetherlam
from Coniston Old Man

Holme Fell

Yew Tree Tarn

Plan your walk

Carlisle

Cockermouth Penrith
Workington Keswick

Whitehaven

Windermere

Kendal

Barrow-in-
Furness Ulverston

Lancaster
Heysham

DISTANCE: 4 miles (6.4km)

TIME: 2 hours

START/END: NY305010
At the foot of
Tibberthwaite Gill

TERRAIN: Strenuous;
rough sections

MAPS:
OS Explorer OL 7;
OS Landranger 90

Route instructions

A Park in the old quarry parking area at the foot of Tilberthwaite Gill, which is reached by a minor road off the A593 Coniston to Ambleside road. From Coniston it is the first turning to the north. From Ambleside it is the second turning on the right after passing the little roadside tarn (Yew Tree Tarn).

B Continue up the road and cross the bridge. Turn sharp right, passing through a narrow gap in the wall and follow the left bank of the river to join a woodland path at a kissing gate.

C At the path junction, bear right and continue on through the wood.

D Turn right onto the minor road and walk along it down to and then alongside the river.

E Turn left just before the bridge. Go up the path by the wall, round and through the gates.

F Turn left at a wall corner up a track. Do not go right, which would take you down to the road. The track passes through a kissing gate after 80yds (75m) and becomes a rough path.

1 View over Yew Tree Tarn.

G The path crosses a fence at a kissing gate. When you get to the big boulders, bear left to climb upwards.

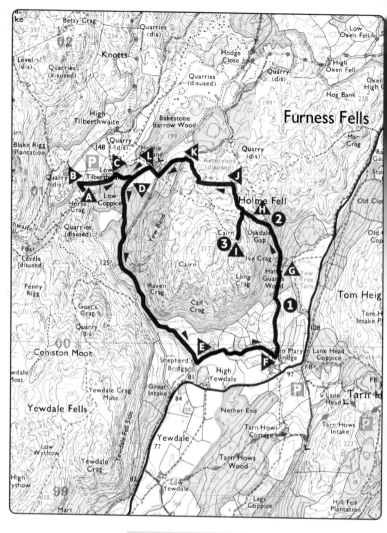

2 View over Langdale Pikes.

H Just after you go through the col (Uskdale Gap) and as the path starts to descend, go left and up to the big stone cairn which

should be visible above. This marks the summit of Ivy Crag.

3 Rest by the cairn and enjoy the view which, by any standards is spectacular.

Holme Fell

Do not be tempted into exploration. There are some dangerous crags to the south. Turn back and return to the path junction at ⓗ. Turn left, going towards the small tarn.

Go left before the tarn, then bear left again to cross the dam of a second tarn. Just after this, bear left once more, passing below a small crag, and after 110yds (100m) bear right to descend to a wall.

At the wall turn left, through the gate and descend. Turn sharp right, down to the cottages and through the gate on to the road.

Walk left past the cottages along the road, and then turn right on the woodland path and retrace your steps to the starting point.

Little Langdale and Wetherlam

> **"** This gentle walk is ideal for a hot summer afternoon stroll, the area is open access common so you can wander freely **"**

This is a lazy walk, ideal for a hot summer day when the common here is loud with skylarks, the air heavy with the antiseptic smell of bog myrtle, and the tarn starred with water lilies. Only a few minutes walk from the Torver to Ulverston road can be found an area of remoteness, marred only a little by the skeins of power lines. This is not typical lakeland. Formerly a forest, it is now a stretch of heath and rough grazing for the hardy sheep which feed on myrtle, juniper, and heather shoots as well as grass. The common is largely open and pathless. There are a few crags and no rough ground here. This gives the area a strange sense of freedom; walk where you like, sit and picnic where you like. The common is managed by the National Park Authority and there is free access.

Torver Low Common

Juniper berries

Route instructions

A The walk starts from the A5084 Torver to Ulverston road 1 mile (1.5km) south of Torver, at Beckstones. There is a layby parking area here opposite a large garage. Turn left out of the car park and walk down the main road.

B 400m down this road, just after a small car park and footpath to the left, turn right off the road and go through a gate onto a path.

C Cross the footbridge over the river and continue on the footpath, which follows the right-hand bank of the beck. (The footbridge was washed away in the floods of November 2009. If it has not been replaced and the river is low it can be forded or crossed on stepping stones, but otherwise you must continue down the road and take the next footpath on the right, after the road bridge).

1 Note the juniper bushes. The local name is 'savins', and the charcoal from it was much used in the manufacture of gunpowder in the district's powder mills. The berries were much valued medicinally for kidney complaints, but of course they are still much used in gin making.

D Turn right, up the small path beside the beck, until you reach the tarn's outflow.

E Turn left, cross the outflow and continue on the

Plan your walk

DISTANCE: 2½ miles (4km)

TIME: 1¼ hours

START/END: SD286930 Layby parking area opposite a large garage on the Coniston to Ulverston road, one mile south of Torver

TERRAIN: Easy; wet sections

MAPS: OS Explorer OL 6; OS Landranger 96

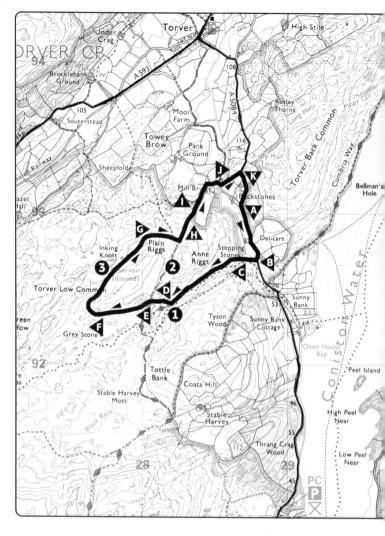

path along the low ridge above the tarn.

2 The level of this tarn was raised artificially to maintain a head of water for a mill below.

▶ **F** 30yds (27m) after passing the end of the tarn bear right on a small path across the marsh, aiming for the prominent crag. Pass underneath the crag, up past the isolated holly bush and continue on the

Torver Low Common

path up to the viewpoint on the top of the hill.

3 Good view over to Coniston Old Man. The crags of Dow are on the left, Goatswater Hause is the dip to the right, and the Old Man is further to the right again.

G From the top, follow the path on and down. At the bottom of the hill, it curves away to the right.

H At the junction of paths by the power line, turn left and follow the path down, underneath the power line.

I Bear right just before the wall and follow the path down, through the gate and down to the old mill.

J After crossing the mill bridge, turn left and up through the gate to follow the path to the road.

K Turn right onto the road with great care as it is a blind corner here. Follow the road a short distance back to the car park.

Old Man of Coniston from Coniston Water

> **❝** From the beacon at the summit of Blawith Fell there is one of the best views of Coniston Water to be seen **❞**

There are beacon points all over Britain and historically they were part of a relatively rapid nationwide communications system. The sites were chosen so as to be visible over a large area and it should therefore follow that they offer the best viewpoints. The beacon on Blawith Fell overlooking the southern end of Coniston Water is a good example, even though it is of modest height at 835 feet (255m). A walk to it would be reward enough, but this route goes by Beacon Tarn, a lovely stretch of water which sits below the fell, and this high area is attractive heather moor. Blawith Fell is part of a common in the care of the National Park so you are free to wander or linger anywhere, but it is recommended to follow the route for the greatest enjoyment.

Summit Cairn, Blawith Fell

Blawith Common & Beacon Tarn

Beacon Tarn

Plan your walk

Carlisle
Cockermouth · Penrith
Workington · Keswick
Whitehaven
Windermere
Kendal
Barrow-in-Furness · Ulverston
Lancaster
Heysham

DISTANCE: 3¾ miles (6km)

TIME: 2 hours

START/END: SD286904 Car parking area on Blawith Common

TERRAIN: Moderate; some wet sections

MAPS:
OS Explorer OL 6;
OS Landranger 96

Route instructions

A Park at a car parking area on Blawith Common. This is an open area just south of Brown Howe on the A5084 Torver to Ulverston road and 1 mile (1.5km) north of Water Yeat. Alternatively there is a larger car park at Brown Howe. Walk down the roadside with care, south towards Water Yeat.

B After 440yds (400m) as the road curves to the left, there is an open area with a stream on your right. A path can be seen ahead going up the hillside through the bracken and you should follow this, crossing the stream shortly after you leave the road. Follow the stream uphill.

C Leave the stream where the ground flattens out and bear right.

D Shortly afterwards bear left, ignoring the path which continues in a northerly direction with the power lines. Continue up and over the hill, going round the side of Slatestone Fell.

E The path descends to a footbridge. Cross the bridge and pick up the path which goes right, and on up beside the beck.

F Follow this up to the tarn and then round the western side of the tarn.

1 Enjoy the quiet tarn. The word 'tarn' has a Norse origin from their word 'tjom'.

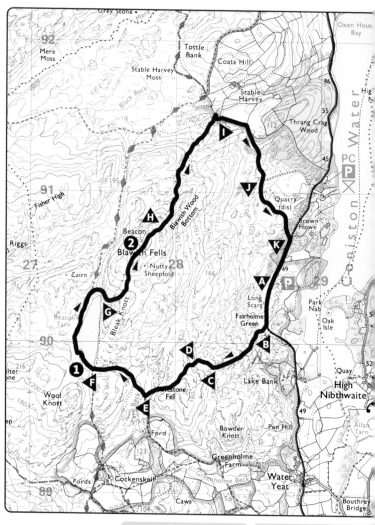

Height has only a little to do with why some stretches of water are called tarns and other lakes. Brother's Water (a lake) for instance, is roughly the same height as this tarn. The practised eye can usually tell the difference; there is less luxurious vegetation around a tarn. The Freshwater Biological Association explains the difference between a lake and a tarn in this way; a lake's characteristic emergent plant is the common reed, while in a tarn it is the bottle

Blawith Common & Beacon Tarn

edge. In the boggy areas around a tarn two small insectiverous plants can be found. They are the sundew with its round red sticky 'dewy' leaves by which it traps insects and the butterwort, which has broad smooth sticky leaves lying flat and looks like a small green starfish. The sundew can easily be missed as it merges so well with the moss.

7 Continue right round the head of the tarn, ignoring the main path which goes up the valley to the north. Then after going down the eastern side of the tarn for a short distance, bear left on a path which climbs up a small valley, initially beside a stream, and joins a larger path. Follow this up to the cairn on the summit of the Beacon.

8 The summit view is mainly eastwards and southwards. Although north-eastwards one can see the whole length of Coniston Water, surely the best view of the lake from any point. The value as a beacon point can be seen. To the south-west is the lump of Black Combe, the site of another beacon which could take signals and pass them on from as far away as Merseyside and the Isle of Man. Far off to the east are the Pennines,

where several beacon points can be seen. To the south is Morecambe Bay and to the north-east there is Helvellyn on the left and the High Street range on the right. To the north-west the view is dominated by the Coniston Old Man range. Dow Crag, the popular rock-climbing cliff is the high point on the left with the lesser peaks of Buck Pike and Brown Pike to the left again. The central fell is the Old Man and Wetherlam is the mass to the right and behind. Natural little rock gardens on the outcrops are charming features of this area.

9 Rejoin the small path and continue on down the hill.

10 At the bottom of the hill turn right onto the tarmac road.

11 When the road bends sharply to the left, go forward onto a footpath (or keep on the road if you have parked at Brown Howe.)

12 When this footpath reaches the main road, turn right and walk back to the starting point.

> **❝** There are some lovely views along the route of this walk from the lakeside path towards the Langdale Pikes **❞**

'Elter' is old Norse for 'swan'. So this is swan lake and aptly named for it is one place visited by Whooper Swans fleeing from their Siberian winter. It is a strangely shaped little lake, fed unusually in its middle reaches at opposite sides by the river Brathay from Little Langdale in the south, and by Great Langdale Beck in the north. Its banks are reedy, unapproachable, and subject to flooding, but there is some valuable grazing land. Therefore on much of the walk described one has to be content with an aggravatingly distant view, but there are compensations. The view from the lakeside path on the south-west, with the Pikes in the background is a classic, and there are two waterfalls, one with an awkward approach, but the other is very close. Needless to say these are at their best after prolonged rain, when some sections of this walk are muddy.

Elterwater & the Waterfalls

Skelwith Bridge

Plan your walk

DISTANCE: 4½ miles (7.2km)

TIME: 2¼ hours

START/END: NY328047 The bridge in Elterwater village

TERRAIN: Moderate; some mud after rain

MAPS:
OS Explorer OL 7; OS Landranger 90

Route instructions

A The walk starts at the bridge in Elterwater village. If the small National Trust car park here is full, there is another car park on the common to the north of the village. Walk south from the bridge on the minor road towards Little Langdale.

B Continue on the road past the Eltermere Inn

C Just after passing the works away to your right, turn right through a gate, signposted 'Colwith', and then immediately afterwards turn left onto a small path. This goes through the wood, parallel to the road and eventually brings you back onto the road. Turn right and continue to a road junction.

D At the road junction, go left and down to the bridge.

E Turn right immediately after crossing the road bridge, and follow a small path beside the stream. This takes you up to Colwith Force.

1 Colwith Force. This pretty fall on the Brathay is about 46ft (14m) in height. The Brathay rises in the Wrynose Pass and until the Local Government reorganisation in 1974, was the boundary between Westmorland to the north, and Lancashire to the south.

F Retrace your steps to the road, turn right and then after another 50yds (45m) turn left through a

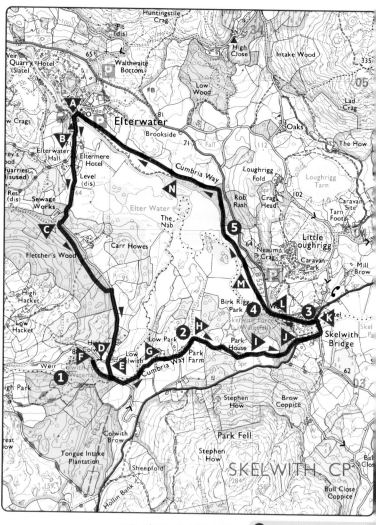

gate, signposted 'Skelwith Bridge'. Follow this path across a field, then climb the steps up a wooded bank and into another field.

G Keep to the right of the farmhouse, up the steps and through the stile.

2 Note the lettering on the stone in the barn wall. This was an apprentice's slab which they could use to develop their skills.

H Go through the farmyard and continue on the track, bearing right.

Elterwater & the Waterfalls

▶ About 100yds (90m) after passing Park House, ignore the track going up to the road, and bear left onto the path which goes into the wood.

▶ Just before you come to a house, take the right fork at a path junction, ignoring the footpath markers going left. Go through the gate in front of the houses and turn left down the road, taking great care as you go round the corner and cross Skelwith Bridge.

▶ After crossing the bridge, turn left by the riverside and go through the slate quarry yard.

3 Showrooms of slate quarry. The slate is formed from volcanic dust laid down in water millions of years ago. It was then subject to enormous pressures. The 'ripple' effect in some of the slate shows well especially when the slate has been sawed and polished. The slate is sawn here with circular saws set with diamond cutters and is much sought after, all over the world, very often as a facing for prestigious buildings. Do not assume that slate lying around here is waste.

▶ Continue on to the falls.

4 Skelwith Force is not high, but through this narrow gap flows all the water from Great and Little Langdale. 'Force' is certainly the right word.

▶ Continue on the path through the fields and into the wood.

5 Just before going into the wood there is a classic viewpoint over the reeds and water to the Langdale Pikes.

▶ At the end of the wood, continue on the riverside path (National Trust property) back to the starting point.

Elterwater

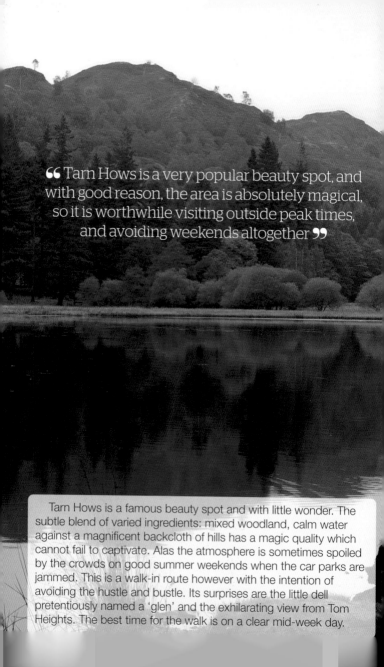

> **"** Tarn Hows is a very popular beauty spot, and with good reason, the area is absolutely magical, so it is worthwhile visiting outside peak times, and avoiding weekends altogether **"**

Tarn Hows is a famous beauty spot and with little wonder. The subtle blend of varied ingredients: mixed woodland, calm water against a magnificent backcloth of hills has a magic quality which cannot fail to captivate. Alas the atmosphere is sometimes spoiled by the crowds on good summer weekends when the car parks are jammed. This is a walk-in route however with the intention of avoiding the hustle and bustle. Its surprises are the little dell pretentiously named a 'glen' and the exhilarating view from Tom Heights. The best time for the walk is on a clear mid-week day.

Glen Mary, Tarn Hows & Tom Heights

Tarn Hows

Route instructions

A Park in the Glen Mary Bridge car park at the bend in the A593 Ambleside to Coniston road 440yds (400m) after you pass Yew Tree Tarn. Start the walk by ascending the path on the north side of Tom Gill.

B There are several paths – keep close to the gill to get the best view of the waterfalls, but be careful if it is very wet.

1 Pass a lovely little waterfall in an intimate setting.

C Come up to the tarn near the dam. Turn right onto the track that crosses the dam, go through the gate and then bear left on the well defined path which

goes round the tarn, signposted at various points as 'Circular Path'.

2 Just after you cross a footbridge at the north end of the tarn you come to a seat and another viewpoint for the tarn. The stone records Sir James and Lady Scott, who gave Tarn Hows to The National Trust in 1930.

D As you are coming down the hill to complete the circuit of the tarn, you have the option of taking one of the small paths up the hill to your right. This will take you up to the cairn and viewpoint on Tom Heights.

3 There are glorious views from all points on this ridge

Plan your walk

Carlisle
Cockermouth Penrith
Workington Keswick
Whitehaven
Windermere
Kendal
Ulverston
Barrow-in-Furness
Lancaster
Heysham

DISTANCE: 3 miles (4.8km)

TIME: 1½ hours

START/END: SD321998 Layby parking south of the little tarn on the roadside between Coniston and Skelwith Bridge

TERRAIN: Moderate; some steep sections

MAPS: OS Explorer OL 7; OS Landranger 97

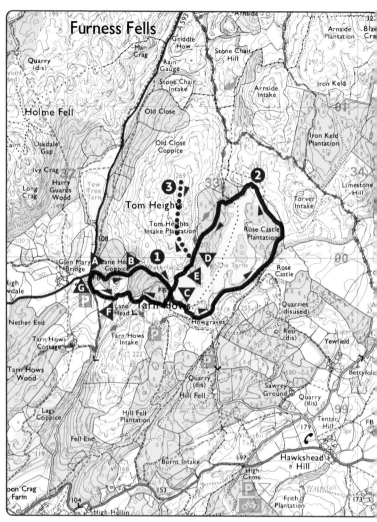

to Coniston Water, through the high fells to Helvellyn and across to Windermere. This is a place to linger. The extraordinary variety of scenery here occurs because this point is in a geological complex. This is the junction between the

Borrowdale Volcanic series which characterises the high fells, and the Silurian slates landscape which is lush with woodlands and without harsh crags. Examples of Silurian slate lie to the south and east of Coniston Water. In between

Glen Mary, Tarn Hows & Tom Heights

the narrow band of Coniston limestone, a grey limestone which geologists might have spotted en route.

E If you have been up to Tom Heights retrace your steps back down to the circular path. Then continue on this to complete your circuit of the tarn, crossing the dam for a second time. Then carry straight on for 55yds (50m) before turning

right onto a stony track which descends through a gate.

F At the junction of paths at Lane Head carry straight on.

G After another 220yds (200m) go through a gate and turn right onto a larger track, which is followed down to the starting point.

Tarn Hows

6 From the viewpoint at Orrest Head there is a superb panorama taking in the central mountains of the Lake District as well as an excellent view of Lake Windermere **9**

Orrest Head is only a short walk from the town of Windermere, yet it offers one of the most rewarding viewpoints in the district, giving an astonishing panorama of the central mountains. It is best done on a clear day. The 'walk goes beyond the Head across the fields and back through the woods of Elleray Bank.

Orrest Head Walk

View from Orrest Head

Route instructions

Plan your walk

> The walk starts from the north side of the A591 opposite the bank and close to its junction with the road down to Bowness and the railway station approach. It begins by going up a tarmac lane.

> After 50yds (46m) ignore the path going off to the left and follow the lane uphill, past the hotel and around the zigzags.

> Just after you pass the blacksmith's cottage, and a bench at a viewpoint over the lake, take the track to the right at a fork.

> When this track reaches a wall, turn right up a path beside the wall.

> Follow this up to a gate in the wall. Turn left through this and up to the summit of Orrest Head.

1 There is a plinth with a view indicator, sometimes alas unreadable through vandalism. Directly and more prominently in front is the Coniston Old Man range (2631ft/802m) with the bulky shoulder of Wetherlam to the right. Further right are the humps of Crinkle Crags with Pike O'Blisco in the foreground.

Beyond, continuing to the right, is the Scafell range, with the highest point in England Scafell Pike (3210ft/978m); nearer is Bowfell (2960ft/902m) and Esk Pike to the right again.

DISTANCE: 2½ miles (4km)

TIME: 1¼ hours

START/END: SD415986 Just north of the town of Windermere; on the A591 road almost opposite to its junction with the road down to Bowness and the railway station approach

TERRAIN: Moderate; some wet patches

MAPS: OS Explorer OL 7; OS Landranger 90

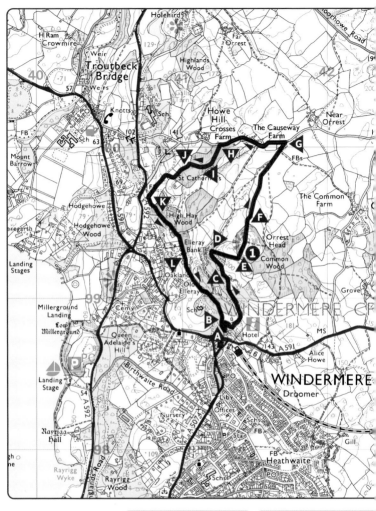

Beyond is Great End, the northern hump of the Scafell range. The Pikes of Langdale are readily recognisable, as are the ridges of High Raise and Ullscarf. Look to the north-west and see the Fairfield range, with Wansfell, above and behind Ambleside. To the north-east is the High Street range. Further east are the Yorkshire Hills. There is an excellent view of the lake, with the woodland facing Claife Heights. The lake appears to be shorter than it is as Belle Isle looks like a southern shoreline.

Orrest Head Walk

▶ Walk north on a path from the summit. Drop down to a stile at a wall junction and then continue across the fields to the right of a wall, until you come to the road.

▶ Go through the gate, turn left onto the road and go down it, passing Causeway Farm.

▶ Another 440yds (400m) after the farm, turn left through a kissing gate into St. Catherine's Wood, owned by the National Trust.

▶ After a footbridge, take the right fork and follow the path down to a kissing gate.

▶ Go through the gate and turn left, following a wall down through another kissing gate and joining a track at the next wall corner.

▶ Before this track reaches the main road, turn left onto a path, signposted 'Orrest Head'.

▶ Follow this path up and through Old Elleray, continuing on it when paths up to Orrest Head bear off up to the left. Go on down and bear right at the tarmac lane and retrace your steps down to the starting point.

View of Lake Windermere from Orrest Head

Photo credits